Hello my fellow ukulele players. Thanks for getting Uk
I'm very excited to share this book with you! The purpose  ....u to enjoy
learning, sharing and playing uplifting music.

After a lot of work, I am very happy with the outcome. I have had much support from my
loving wife Holland and my kids Desmond, Yvette, Leonard, and Charlotte. I hope you enjoy
it as much as I have enjoyed putting it together.

Video Access

If you ordered online, you should have received an email with information to access classes.
If you purchased this book in a retail store, Text "uke" to 888-818-3882 to access members
area, or visit UkuleleHymns.com to sign up for free classes.
If you have further questions, feel free to email me at danny@ukulelehymns.com

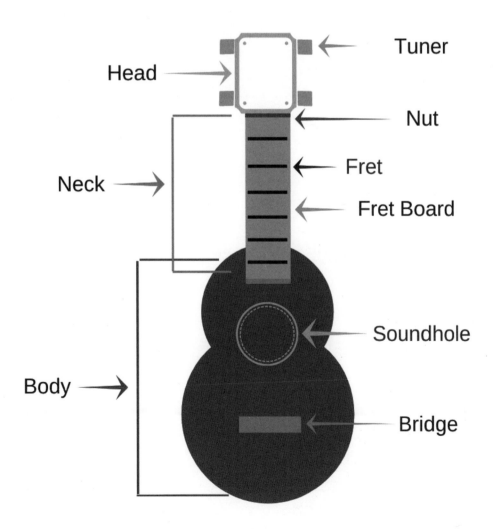

Contents

UkuleleHymns.com

Baptism

Arranged by Daniel E. Heslop

Words: Mabel Jones Gabbot
Music: Crawford Gates; IRI
Used by permission © Ukulele Hymns LLC

Starting Note

Beautiful Savior

Arranged by Daniel E. Heslop

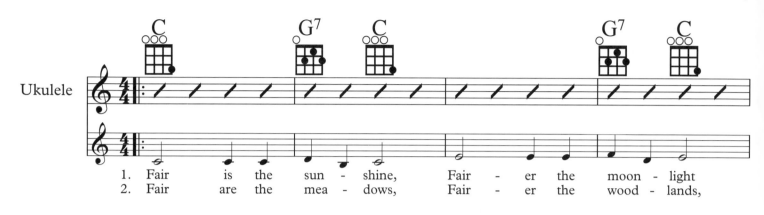

Ukulele

1. Fair is the sun - shine, Fair - er the moon - light
2. Fair are the mea - dows, Fair - er the wood - lands,

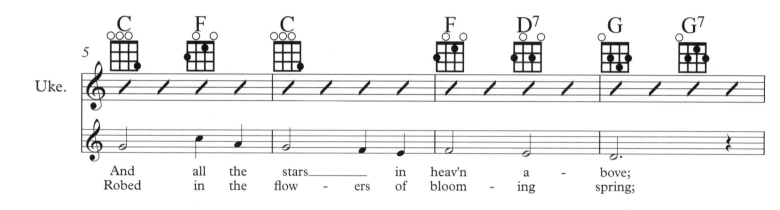

Uke.

And all the stars_____ in heav'n a - bove;
Robed in the flow - ers of bloom - ing spring;

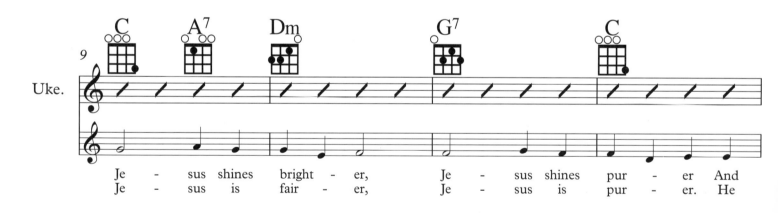

Uke.

Je - sus shines bright - er, Je - sus shines pur - er And
Je - sus is fair - er, Je - sus is pur - er. He

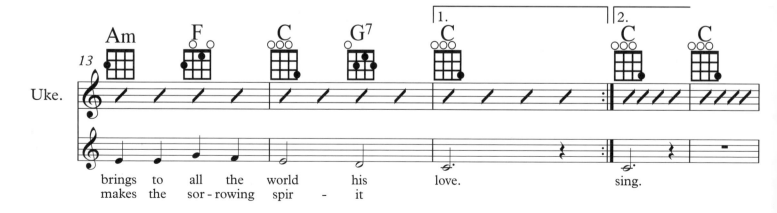

Uke.

brings to all the world his love. sing.
makes the sor - rowing spir - it

Words: Anon 12th century
Music: arr. by Darwin Wolford

3

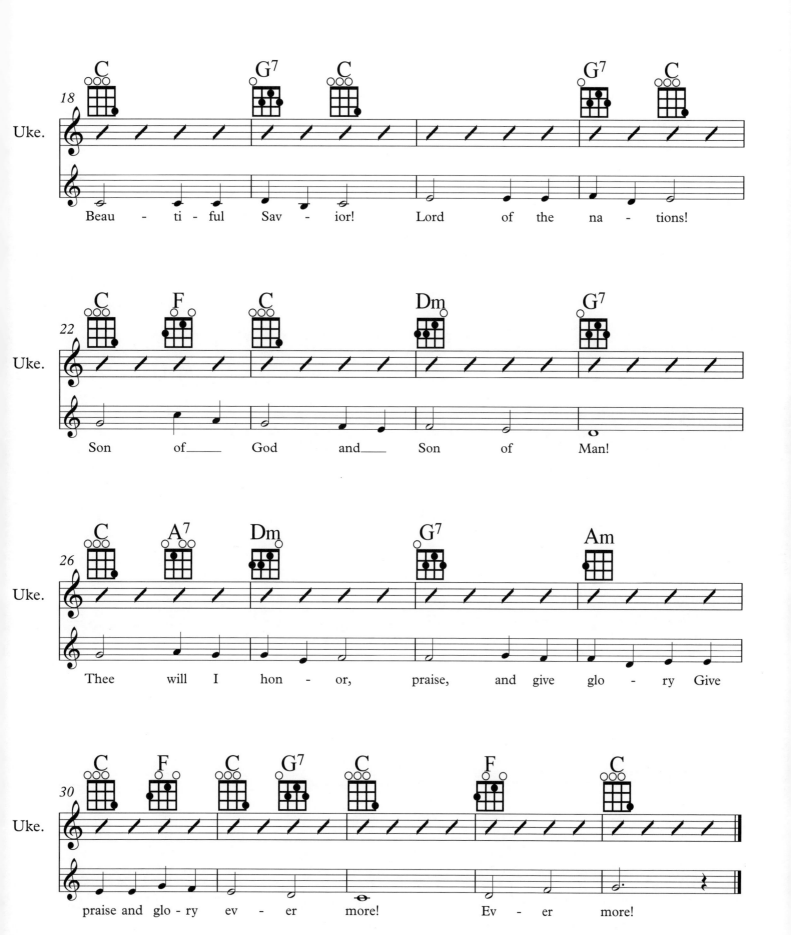

4

Called to Serve

Arranged by Daniel E. Heslop

Words: Grace Gordon
Music: Walter Tyler
© Ukulele Hymns LLC

Families Can Be Together Forever

Arranged by Daniel E. Heslop

Words: Ruth Muir Gardner
Music: Vanja Y. Watkins
Used by permission ©Ukulele Hymns LLC

6

He Sent His Son

Arranged by Daniel E. Heslop

Starting Note

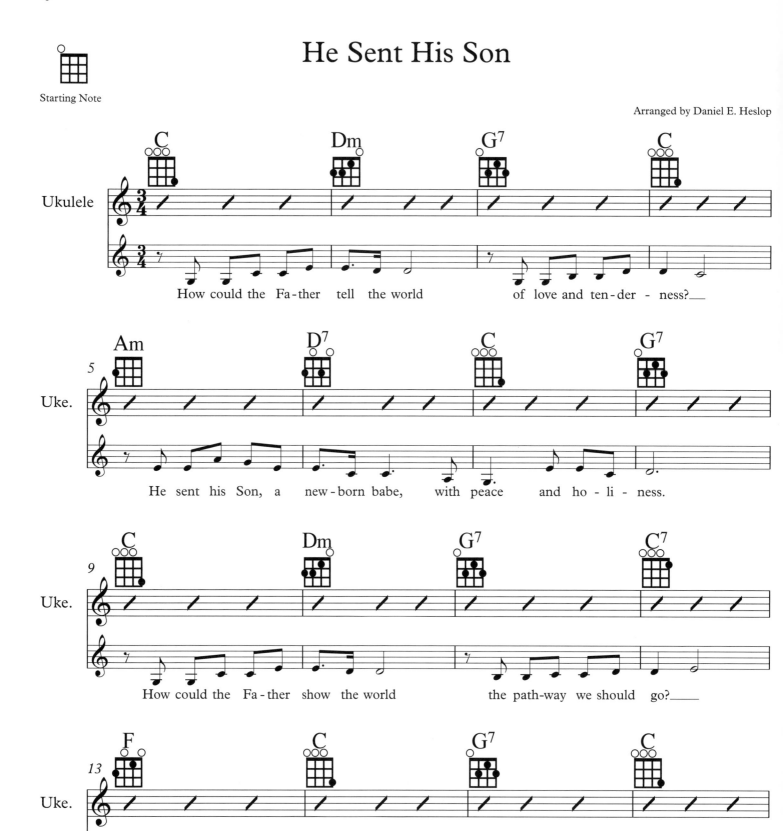

How could the Fa - ther tell the world   of love and ten - der - ness?__

He sent his Son, a new - born babe, with peace and ho - li - ness.

How could the Fa - ther show the world   the path - way we should go?__

He sent his Son to walk with men   on earth, that we may know.

Words: Mabel Jones Gabbott
Music: Michael Finlinson Moody
Used by permission ©Ukulele Hymns LLC

I Feel My Savior's Love

Arranged by Daniel E. Heslop

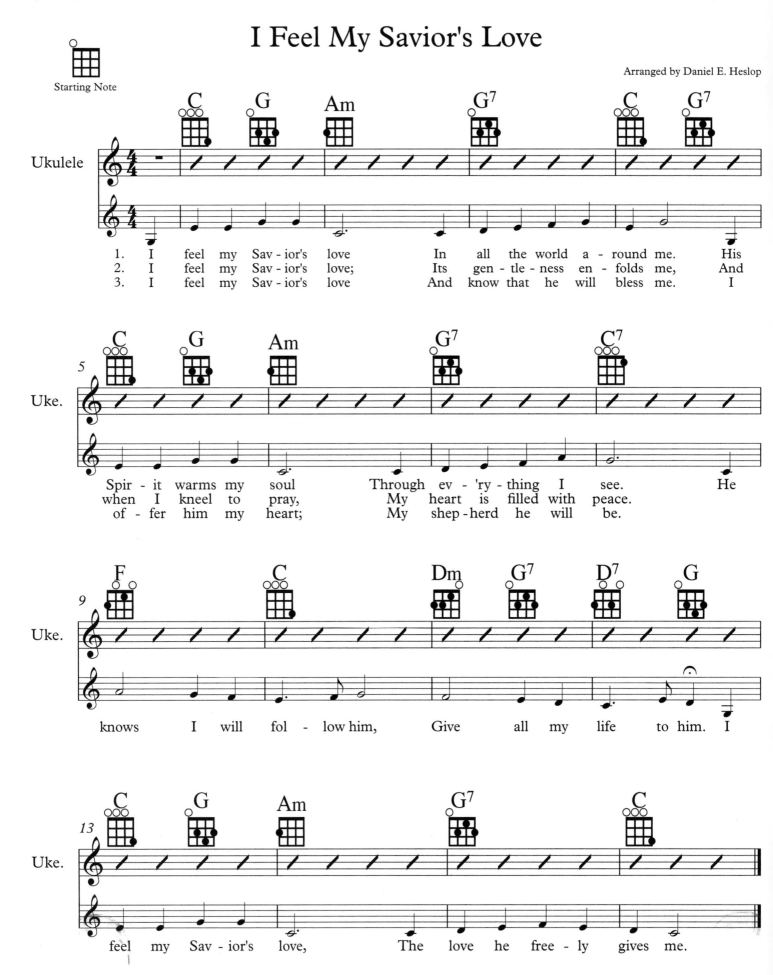

Words: Ralph Rodgers, K. Newell Dayley, and Laurie Huffman
Music: K. Newell Dayley
Used by permission ©Ukulele Hymns LLC

I Love to See the Temple

Arranged by Daniel E. Heslop

Starting Note

Words and Music: Janice Kapp Perry
Used by Permission © Ukulele Hymns LLC

I'll Walk with You

Arranged by Daniel E. Heslop

In the Leafy Treetops

Arranged by Daniel E. Heslop

Starting Note

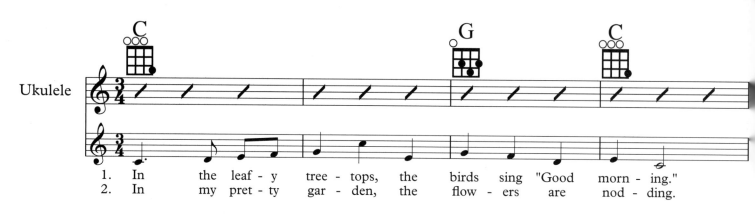

1. In the leaf - y tree - tops, the birds sing "Good morn - ing."
2. In my pret - ty gar - den, the flow - ers are nod - ding.

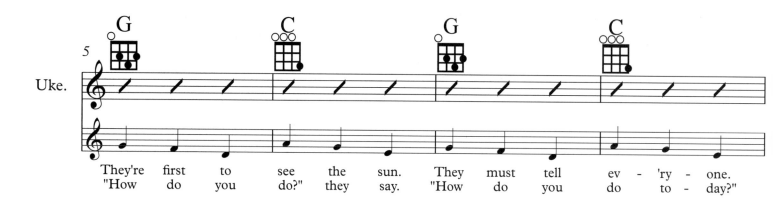

They're first to see the sun. They must tell ev - 'ry - one.
"How do you do?" they say. "How do you do to - day?"

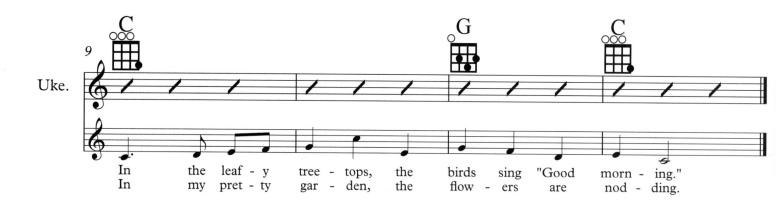

In the leaf - y tree - tops, the birds sing "Good morn - ing."
In my pret - ty gar - den, the flow - ers are nod - ding.

Love Is Spoken Here

Arranged by Daniel E. Heslop

Words & Music: Janice Kapp Perry
Used by permission ©Ukulele Hymns LLC

Love One Another

Arranged by Daniel E. Heslop

Starting Note

As I have loved you, Love one an-oth-er.

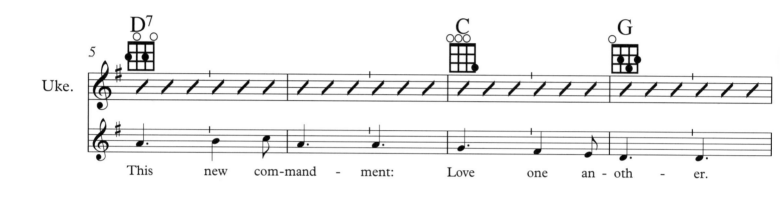

This new com-mand - ment: Love one an-oth - er.

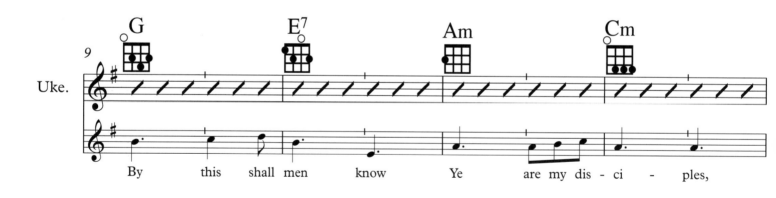

By this shall men know Ye are my dis-ci - ples,

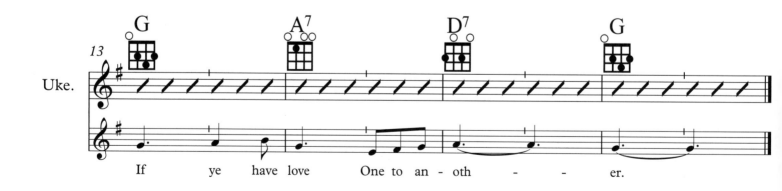

If ye have love One to an-oth - - er.

Words & Music: Luacine Clark Fox
©2004, 1978 by Intellectual Reserve, Inc.
©Ukulele Hymns LLC

Samuel Tells of the Baby Jesus

Arranged by Daniel E. Heslop

1. Said Sam - u - el, "With - in five years A night will be as day, And
2. A - cross the sea, in Beth - le - hem, Lord Je - sus came to earth As

Ba - by Je - sus will be born In a land far, far a - way."
Sam - u - el had pro - phe - sied, And an - gels sang His birth.

Ho - san - na! Ho - san - na! Oh, let us glad - ly sing. How

bless - ed that our Lord was born; Let earth re - ceive her King!

Words: Mabel Jones Gabbott
Music: Grietje Terburg Rowley
Use by permission ©Ukulele Hymns LLC

Search, Ponder, and Pray

Arranged by Daniel E. Heslop

Teach Me to Walk in the Light

arting Note

Arranged by Daniel E. Heslop

1. Teach me to walk in the light of his love;
2. Come, lit - tle child, and to - geth - er we'll learn
3. Fa - ther in Heav - en, we thank thee this day

Teach me to pray to my Fa - ther a - bove;
Of his com - mand - ments, that we may re - turn
For lov - ing guid - ance to show us the way.

Teach me to know of the things that are right;
Home to his pres - ence, to live in his sight
Grate - ful, we praise thee with songs of de - light!

Teach me, teach me to walk in the light.
Al - ways, al - ways to walk in the light.
Glad - ly, glad - ly we'll walk in the light.

Words & Music: Clara W. McMaster
Used by permission ©Ukulele Hymns LLC